Introduction

Have you ever imagined what it would be like to make over $2,000 - $30,000/month while you are doing things you enjoy, while you travel, and even while you sleep?

This way of making money appeared with the birth of the Internet, and it extended quickly and continues to expand today. The Internet is growing bigger and bigger and new entrepreneurs and smart people are taking advantage of it as we speak.

This whole concept is called 'Passive Income' and trust me, the 21st century will be the century of passive income. This century will be a historical start for new entrepreneurs like you or me. The Internet has provided us with some tools that didn't even exist a few decades ago – new ways of viral marketing.

Several decades ago, the concept of 'Passive income' wasn't so popular, even though there were some methods that could have brought money passively, like real estate (through rent payments).

Chapter 1: What is Amazon KDP?

Amazon is currently the biggest retailer in the world, it is the 'everything' online store. Amazon is exactly like a search engine, it's the place where millions of people have their credit cards attached and come to buy products.

Also, Amazon provides outstanding opportunities for marketers, authors, resellers, and product developers. On Amazon, you can become an entrepreneur easily using 3 different methods: Amazon KDP, Amazon FBA, and Amazon Associates.

Amazon Associates is Amazon's affiliate program. You will earn commissions by promoting products from Amazon. *Amazon FBA*, or 'Fulfilled by Amazon', is for selling physical products on Amazon - you provide Amazon your product and they wrap it, sell it, and ship it for you. You only collect the royalties. *Amazon KDP*, or Kindle Direct Publishing, is exclusively for authors and publishers, allowing you to self-publish eBooks on the Kindle store.

Here, I will cover literally everything I know, experienced, heard, and seen about KDP. You will find that this guide is the most complex and complete one on the whole Kindle store.

I can assure you that Kindle Publishing is the fastest way to start making money online. You write a book, you publish it, and within a few hours, or days, you will see royalties coming to your account. Of course, there is a lot of work to do before you can see thousands of dollars rolling in.

You don't have to be a scientist to release a nonfiction book. You don't have to be a native English speaker to create an outstanding high-quality book. You don't have to write about science fiction to make money. All you need is time, passion for the subjects you write about, and a lot of perseverance.

The most interesting thing about Kindle Publishing is that you don't need money to get started. All you need is an idea, the content, a cover, which you can make by yourself or for free (using Amazon cover creator), and you are done. Well, this is just as a beginning if you don't have any money. In this book, I will talk about both perspectives: high quality, which involves some investment, and free/cheaper methods to make money fast.

What I am saying is this:

If you're the type of person who is looking for a way to make money online passively, if you are the type of person who wants more freedom, if you don't want to go to your stressful job one more day, or if you are the type of person who wants their own business, then this type of business is for you.

I am realistically telling you that within 3 months, you will be making $500/month, within 6 months, you will be making $800 to $1,000 and within 2 years, you will easily be making at least $5,000/month.

There are publishers who have managed to earn over $30,000 month without being novelists or popular authors.

The main secrets in making money on Kindle are:

-Quality
-Quantity
-Marketing

To become a real bestseller, you need to combine quality with quantity and marketing. The more quality books you release and you promote, the more money you will be making.

If you are willing to create short Kindle books that have 20-30 pages, poor content, lots of mistakes, and a basic cover...I am sorry, but you won't be making any money or if you are making any, it will be for short term (1-2 months).

A successful Kindle publishing business has to be based on *quality*.

Chapter 2: Where to start?

Many people want to get into this business, but they don't know where to start. The answer is simple. You start by picking a profitable niche and you start researching.

Niche Test

First of all, you need to decide what you would like to write about in your future book. If you want to get the best results out of your book, I highly recommend you write about a niche, a subject, that you would be interested in. Write a book that you would buy yourself.

To see if a specific niche is selling, you first need to go to http://amazon.com and see the "Bestsellers" of the category you are aiming to write for. For example, you have decided to write about sports

(Exercise & Fitness), you will need to go to the "Bestsellers" list and you will see the top 100 free and top 100 paid in different   categories.

Popular Features

Kindle Unlimited

Kindle Best Sellers

Kindle Singles

Kindle Select 25

The Amazon Book Review

New York Times® Best Sellers

Editors' Picks

Short Reads

Kindle First

Kindle Worlds

Spanish eBooks

Then, what you need to do is to go to the smallest subcategory for exercise and fitness and pick one of the smallest categories. I have picked "Health & Fitness" as the main category, then I have picked "Exercise & Fitness" as the next subcategory and then "Aerobics" the smallest subcategory. From there, you can see the top 100 paid books from that

‹ Any Department
  ‹ Kindle Store
    ‹ Kindle eBooks
      ‹ Health, Fitness & Dieting
        Exercise & Fitness
        (Aerobics)
        Running & Jogging
        Yoga

category.

The bestselling book from that category is ranked at #13,000, which isn't too bad. This means that the author is selling around 15-20 units daily. If you look at other bestselling subcategories, you will see that the #1 rank in that subcategory will be between 5,000 and 30,000.

If your book gets to #1 in the subcategory, it will then climb to the other higher categories, which would be "Exercise and fitness". I advise you to go from the smallest subcategory to the biggest because it will be easier for you to outrank the other competitors. Competition is low on the smallest subcategories compared to the main category. If the book you are writing will be too broad, something like "Fitness for all", this would be extremely hard to rank high in. Think big, but start small, from the smallest subcategories. To sum up, the final "*Niche Test*" you have to do before you decide what you will be writing about, look at the first 1-2 books from the category and then look at number 60 and 80 from top 100. If their rank is higher than #100,000 (a higher rank means that you are selling less, I will cover more about ranking in a dedicated chapter).

In my example, the first book from "Aerobics" is ranked at #13,000 and the 60th book is ranked at #294,000, so this niche isn't too profitable, but you can give it a try.

Competition

As soon as you decide what to write about, you will need to come up with a title. Search the title using Amazon's search bar and see how many results you get with similar titles. Identify your competitors and see how they are doing with their book – how many pages they have, how the cover looks, how many reviews they have, when the book was published, and what rank they have. If you have noticed that they are all doing well, and they have books that are at least 6 months old, and you think that you can come up with a better book than theirs, then go for it. *Tip #1 – Always identify your primary competitors and make a better book than theirs – a more attractive cover, create more content (more pages), create a paperback version of your book (I will discuss this later), an Audible ACX (I will also discuss this later) and make it visible.*

Demand

Before you start writing a book, figure out if that book will be profitable long-term. Look for books that are old (1-2 years since they were published) and look at their ranks. If they are selling good, then the niche of your future book is profitable. There are books on Amazon that sell well only for a limited time. Of course, the quality of the book has a crucial influence on the demand of the book and even in the niche.

Market

There is a market for everything, but the question is, how *big* is the market for your book? To find out, go to Amazon's search bar and type the title/keyword from the book you are going to create. When you search for a keyword, you shouldn't have more than 2,000 results or less than 500.

A number lower than 500 results mean that there is a low market for that book and you won't make enough money from it. More than 2,000 results means that your niche is too broad and it will be hard to outrank your competitors.

Chapter 3: Understanding the Audience

Before you start getting into the publishing business, you first need to understand what you are willing to write about, what topics you like, who you are writing for, and what your readers want from your books. Before you publish your first book, you have to see yourself as a reader – what would you like to see in a book before you buy it? Make a list with some ideas that you think your future readers would like, and then take the following things into consideration:

1. Book length - Write at least 10,000 - 15,000 words for each book. Please, just *please,* don't upload 15-20 page books on Amazon and call yourself an author! 15,000 words converts into a 100-page book with a 6 x 9 size, 10,000 words convert into a 90-page book with a 5 x 8 size (I will cover this more in the CreateSpace chapter).

2. Proofread and edit your work - You don't want to have any spelling or grammar mistakes into your book, even if no book is perfect. I am sure you have seen, or will see, an error in my book and it won't make you feel comfortable, my apologies for that. As I said, no book is perfect, but you need to send your book to professional proofreaders to have a look at your book before you publish it.

3. Topic - Choose a topic that you would love to write about, for example, I like writing about business. I have always wanted to build my own online business, and I like writing about business, marketing, or guides (like this one you are reading now). I wouldn't like to write about diabetes, erectile dysfunction, or skin conditions. Maybe other authors don't like writing about business because it seems harder for them, who knows? The essential idea here is to understand that the best books you will ever create will be about things you enjoy doing.

4. Make everything professional - Description, cover, everything. Don't just make a cover in Paint and upload it on Kindle, it's embarrassing. If you don't have the skills, hire a freelancer, pay him $10, and get an excellent, good looking cover.

5. Be natural - Write what readers are looking for. Make sure to deliver what you promised your readers in the title. Don't come up with a misleading title because you will get negative reviews and you will lose sales.

6. Write about what you love – It's a lot easier for you and a lot better for readers if you write about something you love and you are familiar with. You will also be able to write more content with excellent quality.

Chapter 4: Title and Subtitle

Titles and subtitles are an essential piece of your puzzle. It's basically the first words that your customers will see and they have an excellent influence on your sales.

Title

1. **Keywords** – Make sure your title contains keywords that are different from the ones you choose when you upload the book. If your title contains keywords, it will be easier to find in the searches and it will rank higher.
2. **Description** – Your title needs to be descriptive and clean at the same time. Carefully describe what the book contains but don't make the title cover the whole picture.

3. **Include benefits** – Your title needs to give your customer at least one benefit. For example, "Get rid of fat", "Learn Photoshop", "Become financially free", "Become an affiliate". These are benefits and you need to include at least one in your title.

Subtitle

The subtitle also needs to contain keywords and to be descriptive. Write as many keywords as you can in the subtitle to rank higher in the searches.

Series

Choose an eye-catching title for your series' title that is also a keyword. Just remember, the more keywords you have, the higher you rank. Include them anywhere you can.

Examples of suitable titles

- *Paleo Slow Cooker – 100+ Delicious Recipes for a Healthy Life and Weight Loss.*
  You have a keyword (Paleo Slow Cooker) and 2 benefits (have a healthy life and lose weight) and it's also descriptive.
- *Job Escape – How to Successfully Retire and Be Financially Free without Compromises*
- *Work from Home – How to Build an Online Business in 7 Days That Really Works*

Examples of bad titles

- *Job Escape*
- *How to Build a Business*
- *Weight Loss*
- *Self-Motivation Techniques*

Note - If you want to invest a lot of money in a book that has ultimate quality and you want to use a broad keyword in your title (to have a big text ratio for your keyword – see the keyword chapter), then you can make something like "Online Marketing Complete Guide" – it attracts you, you know what it is about (or you can guess) and you have a great text ratio. If you don't invest in books like this, then use titles that are more descriptive and have more keywords.

Chapter 5: Cover

If you want to encourage people to click on your book and buy it, you need to create a cover that is professional, clean, and attractive.

Colors - Try to use vivid colors as background – red, blue, green, yellow – and the title needs to be in contrast with these colors. Don't put a dark red title on a light red background, it won't be visible. *Title* - Make the title *big* enough so it can be seen even on smartphones. If someone sees your book but can't read the title, many people will not click to read it, they will simply scroll to the next book.

Fonts - Use professional fonts that look nice such as Cambria, Impact, Calson Pro, etc. (Don't use Times New Roman!)

Dimensions - Make the size dependent on the size of the document. For instance, if you have a 6 x 9 document (formatted), use a 6 x 9 size for your cover. Generally, Amazon recommends a size that has a 1. ratio, but 6 x 9 or 5 x 8 inches is excellent.

Resolution - Make your covers at 300 dpi. It's the minimum resolution for which the cover won't be blurry when printing. This is recommended if you upload your book on CreateSpace.

Format - Use JPEG or TIFF for Kindle and PDF for CreateSpace.

Back - Create a back cover for your book (for CreateSpace)

Spine - The spine is influenced by the number of pages. (CreateSpace) - For black & white pages - 0. 02252 inches x (number of pages) or 0. 025 inches x (number of pages) for full color pages.

Bleed - For black & white pages - use a 0. 25" bleed for spine, width, and height

Example of dimensions - For a 6 x 9 book with 100 pages, your width will be Bleed

+ Back Cover Trim Size + Spine Width + Front Cover Trim Size + Bleed = 0. 25" + 6" + (number of pages) x 0. 02252 + 0. 25" = 12. 753" (Width). For Height - 0. 25" + 9" + 0. 25" = 9. 5"

Glossy or Matte - It's your choice; I prefer glossy.

Example of Kindle covers (5 x 8 - JPEG)

Example of CreateSpace cover (PDF)

"The internet has become a goldmine in our days, and the truth is that anyone can start mining at any time. With the right tools and mindset, the internet can easily become your daily playground. Affiliate marketing is one of the most popular ways to earn money passively with the help of this precious tool. Amazon Associates is one of the biggest players when it comes to affiliate marketing. There isn't any platform as advanced, as good and as fast as Amazon - you will find everything profitable, easy to learn and enjoyable at the same time.
Start your online career now and become an affiliate!"

AMAZON ASSOCIATES

AFFILIATE PROGRAM

RYAN STEVENS

Chapter 6: Publishing On Other Platforms

If you want to expand your sales, a good strategy is to upload your book(s) on other platforms. I honestly haven't upload any book on other platforms yet, but I will and the first one will be a perma-free book (more about this in the perma-free book chapter).

It's not recommended to upload on multiple platforms from the very beginning, as you can't take advantage of KDP Select (exclusive program) and you won't be allowed to promote your book on Amazon. At first, you have to release several book (a series of books) on a similar topic, promote them all, and after 3 or 6 months, when the KDP Select period (90 days) is over, upload 1 or 2 books from that series on other platforms. Although you can't promote the books you upload on other platforms, the others from the same series will promote the others, too. In the same manner, the books you upload on the related platforms will promote the other books you have on Amazon. This is a good strategy to expand your visibility, increase your rank, and make more money from the books you already have.

Sales on other platforms are not as good as on Kindle, but they are similar. Some authors claim that for every 100 books sold on Kindle (fiction), they also sold around 30-50 books on Nook and Smashwords, which is excellent.

Other platforms to submit your book:

- Smashwords
- Nook (Barnes & Noble)
- iTunes (Apple)

- CreateSpace (Amazon)
- Google Play

Chapter 7: Audible ACX

Many people today prefer to listen to something instead of reading. This can be done while you walk, while you run, while you do something else, or even while you sleep.

Generally, audiobooks go well with both fiction and nonfiction (business, how-to, guides, etc.).

Children's books have the biggest advantage with Audible. There is no need to read them a bedtime story every evening, you just give them a phone or tablet and they can listen to however many stories they want to until they fall asleep.

The amount of money you can earn from Audible ACX is from 10 to 20% of your total Kindle sales.

Note – Audible ACX is available only for publishers and authors from the US and UK (residents).

How It Works

Calling all authors, narrators, agents, publishers and studio pros: ACX needs you!

Are you ready to revolutionize the audiobook creation process? Here are step-by-step instructions of how ACX works for you

Authors

Get your title up and out there:

○ Confirm your rights

○ Create your title profile

○ Find a Producer

○ Make a deal to get your audiobook produced!

To set up an audiobook, go to http://acx.com and sign up with them. You will need professional narrators to create your audiobook and you can find them on Fiverr.com, http://Freelancer.com, or directly on ACX. Prices are high as it requires professionals to deliver good quality work. You can narrate the books on your own, but I *don't* recommend that. They require professionals.

Expect these services to be expensive. Professionals will charge you $10-$25 for every 100-150 words, so for a 10,000-word book, you will pay around $1,350 or more. Some narrators will work with you only if you share the profits with them (don't do that).

Audiobooks work well if you have good quality books that already sell. Invest in an Audible ACX format only when the fees of creating one will cover the net profits from the book you have. If you do this from the beginning, you might lose money.

Chapter 8: Signing Up with Amazon

To become a self-publisher on Amazon, you first need to go at http://kdp. amazon.com and create an account. Complete all the fields carefully, and make sure to use your *real* name and information because you will attach credit cards to your name.

Tax Withhold Rates

Before you can see your dashboard and start publishing, you need to complete the Tax Interview.

You will need to complete some fields. Based on this, you will get an applicable

Tax Withholding Rate, which is from 0 to 30%.

- US residents pay 15% withholding rate for sales made in the US store and 0% on the others.
- UK residents pay 0% withholding rate.
- Countries that are in tax treaties with US pay 10% withholding rate.
- Countries that are not in tax treaties with US pay 30% withholding rate.

Payment methods

You have 2 main options to choose from:

- Check payment – As soon as you meet the minimum threshold for each currency ($, EUR, and GBP) you will receive a paycheck.
- Direct deposit – Create a bank account if you don't have one and

attach the bank account ID to your KDP account.

Note – Choose direct deposit as it's faster and cheaper. Check payments will be commissioned supplementary.

Getting paid

Getting paid from Amazon will take place every 60 days for each month. This means that for every month in which you make some sales, you will see the money from that month after 60 days. For example, if you make $500 in January, you will get paid at the end of March.

Amazon will send you *Accounts Payables* on the 20th of each month and will tell you that you will receive your money starting with 29th in 2 to 5 business days. I usually go to take my money on 3rd or 4th of the new upcoming month to be sure.

So, if you make money in January, you get your money at the beginning of April, for the month of February, you take your money at the beginning of May, etc. January -> April

February -> May

March -> June

April -> July

May -> August

June -> September

July -> October

August -> November

September -> December

October -> January

November -> February

December -> March

I know, it's annoying to wait that long, especially if you are waiting for your first payment, but the good news is that when you take $1,000, for example, you know that you have another 2 payments pending and you can rely on that money.

Chapter 9: Dashboard

In this place, you will find out how many sales, borrows, free units, and how much money you made. You can see your activity for up to 90 days, but the dashboard will show you on the last 30 days as standard. It also has a few features such as "last 2 weeks" or "month to date" and lets you choose individual days to see your activity.

It looks like this:

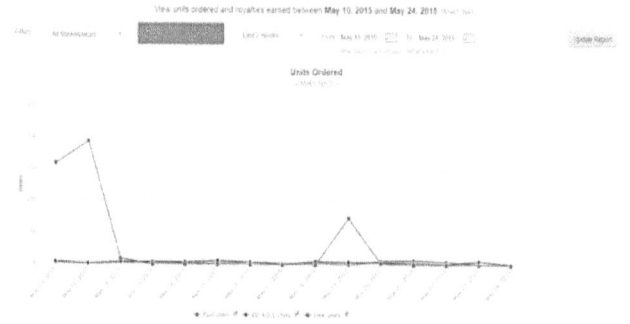

- Green line – Free units (during KDP Select free promotion days)
- Blue line – Borrows
- Red line – Paid units

You can click on the green line box and remove the free units to see your daily sales more accurately.

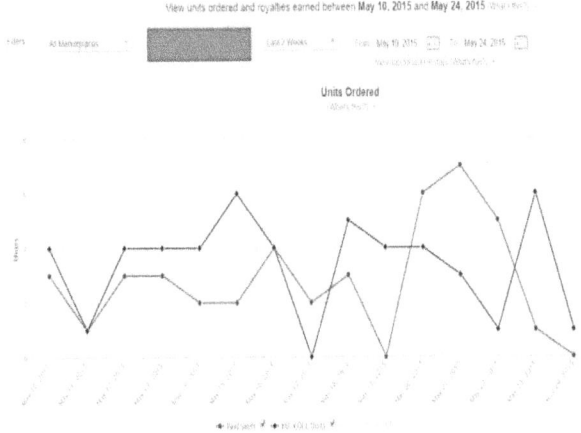

Below these graphs, you can check your royalties (gross income, withhold rates don't apply here). The royalties are from all Amazon stores, which include US, UK,

Mexico, Canada, Australia, Brazil, Spain, Italy, Germany, Japan, India, Netherlands, and France. When the payment is processed, all the royalties that have a different currency will be automatically converted into US, EUR, or GBP, depending on where you live.

Marketplace	Royalty
Amazon.com	547.75 USD
Amazon.co.uk	64.42 GBP
Amazon.de	6.74 EUR
Amazon.fr	0.33 EUR
Amazon.es	1.72 EUR
Amazon.it	5.01 EUR
Amazon.nl	0.00 EUR
Amazon.co.jp	0.00 JPY
Amazon.in	556.51 INR
Amazon.ca	27.64 CAD
Amazon.com.br	0.00 BRL
Amazon.com.mx	0.00 MXN
Amazon.com.au	19.29 AUD

Royalties from this small table are only from paid units. Borrows are paid separately at the end of each month.

Beneath this table, you have links to CreateSpace, Audible ACX, Community, and Contact Amazon.

Chapter 10: KDP Select Tools

Many books on Amazon wouldn't sell if Amazon didn't come up with some tools for publishers. All these tools are included in an exclusive promotional program called KDP Select.

Introducing KDP Select

Take advantage of KDP Select, an optional program that makes your book exclusive to Kindle and eligible for the following benefits

- **Reach more readers** - With each 90-day enrollment period, your book will appear in Kindle Unlimited in the U.S., U.K., Italy, Spain, Germany, France, Brazil, Mexico and Canada and the Kindle Owners' Lending Library (KOLL) in the U.S., U.K., Germany, France, and Japan which can help readers discover your book
- **Earn more money** - Every time your book is selected and read past 10% from Kindle Unlimited or borrowed from KOLL, you'll earn your share of the monthly KDP Select Global Fund. You can also earn a 70% royalty for sales to customers in Japan, Brazil, India and Mexico.
- **Maximize your sales potential** - Choose from two promotional tools including Kindle Countdown Deals, time-bound promotional discounts for your book available on Amazon.com and Amazon.co.uk, while earning royalties, or Free Book Promotion, where readers can get your book free for a limited time

Learn more

☐ Enroll this book in KDP Select

By checking this box, you are enrolling in KDP Select for 90 days. Books enrolled in KDP Select must not be available in digital format on any other platform during their enrollment. If your book is found to be available elsewhere in digital format, it may not be eligible to remain in the program. See the KDP Select Terms and Conditions and KDP Select FAQs for more information

The advantages:

1. You can earn 70% royalty on most of the stores (you would've earned 35% otherwise).
2. You can promote your book for free 5 days every 90 days.

3. You can promote your book using Countdown deal 7 days every 90 days.

4. People can borrow your book and you earn a royalty for that (around $1.00 for each borrow).

5. You get more visibility and more sales.

Free Promotion Days

While you promote the book for 5 days, you need to do your best to acquire as many downloads as possible. The more you get, the higher you rank in Amazon's search engine, more people will come across your book, and the more sales you'll make. In the next chapters, I will include some strategies for promoting a book and some resources.

Kindle Countdown Deals

You can drop the price up to 7 days and get a royalty of 70% (more about pricing later) and increase your rank. I use this feature rarely because I prefer the free promotion days. If you already have a decent rank, a decent number of reviews, and you are a popular Author, then you can try out a Kindle Countdown deal.

Run a Price Promotion on Amazon

Sign your book up for one of the following promotional programs. Only one promotional program can be enabled per enrollment period. Please select either Kindle Countdown Deals or Free Book Promotion.

- Kindle Countdown Deal Learn more
- Free Book Promotion Learn more

⚠ This book is currently ineligible for a Kindle Countdown Deal (Why?)

Note - You can use Free Promotion days OR Kindle Countdown Deals. You can't use them both, but you can switch between them every 90 days.

To enroll in KDP Select, you need to click the box "enroll" at the top of the page. What you need to know is that KDP Select is Amazon's exclusive program, so you will not be allowed to publish your book on other platforms during the enrollment (90 days). If you want to make money from other platforms, too, you can promote your book on Kindle for 3 or 6 months and then to quit the program. KDP Select is for each individual book so you can enroll however many you want.

Chapter 11: Kindle Unlimited

I am pretty sure that you have noticed that most of the books from Kindle can be borrowed for free (for Prime members or Kindle Unlimited members). In the dashboard, you will see a blue line that represents these borrows.

You will probably think, *Hmm, if I borrow a book, does it mean I am giving it away for free?* No, not at all. In some cases, it's really profitable and I will explain why.

kindleunlimited

Unlimited Reading. Unlimited Listening. Any Device.

Enjoy the freedom to explore over 800,000 titles and thousands of audiobooks on any device for just $9.99 a month.

Give the gift of Kindle Unlimited

Kindle Unlimited subscribers pay $9.99/month and they can read an *unlimited* number of books enrolled in KDP Select (most books are enrolled).

Prime members also pay $100/year and they have several advantages for that - rushed or free shipping, they can watch movies, listen to music, unlimited cloud storage, and they can also borrow your books. Borrowers can "keep" the book in their library for fourteen days and then it will automatically "retract" or delete.

Amazon collects the money from Kindle Unlimited subscribers and a small part of Prime members and they create the Global Fund for KU, which is updated each month.

The Global Amount is usually $3 Million, but Amazon adds funds at the end of each month to supplement the base fund. As many new users have joined KU, the price for a borrow has significantly dropped, so Amazon supplements the fund to increase the royalty for a borrow. As they said, they won't allow a borrow to decrease lower than $1.

That amount is divided by the total number of borrows and there's your money. Generally, a borrow is now from $5 to $1, depending on how many books have been borrowed. It's really annoying now because a year ago, a borrow was somewhere around $2, and it slowly dropped. Books that are priced at $0.99 have an advantage. If a reader purchases a $0.99 book, you get $0.50 royalty and if a reader borrows your book, you get $1 (on average).

Here is a screenshot from my reports regarding a KOLL (borrow) unit.

Net Units Sold or KU/KOLL Units*[1]	Royalty Type[2]	Transaction Type[3]	Avg List Price without VAT (USD)	Average File Size (MB)	Avg Offer Price without VAT (USD)	Average Delivery Cost (USD)	Royalty (USD)
	38%	Standard	0.99	0.17	N/A	N/A	1.40
	N/A	Free - Promotion	1.52	0.17	0.00	N/A	0.00
	N/A	Free - Promotion	1.84	0.17	0.00	N/A	0.00
	70%	Standard	2.99	0.51	2.99	0.06	8.18
	N/A	KU/KOLL Units	N/A	N/A	N/A	N/A	1.34
	N/A	Free - Promotion	2.95	0.51	0.00	N/A	0.00
	35%	Standard	0.99	0.18	N/A	N/A	3.18
	35%	Standard	0.99	0.19	N/A	N/A	3.85
	N/A	KU/KOLL Units	N/A	N/A	N/A	N/A	2.67
	N/A	KU/KOLL Units	N/A	N/A	N/A	N/A	4.81
	N/A	Free - Promotion	0.99	0.19	0.00	N/A	0.00
	70%	Standard	2.94	0.53	2.94	0.08	16.95
	N/A	KU/KOLL Units	N/A	N/A	N/A	N/A	2.67
	70%	Standard	3.99	1.10	3.99	0.17	42.75
	N/A	KU/KOLL Units	N/A	N/A	N/A	N/A	8.02
	N/A	Free - Promotion	3.97	1.10	0.00	N/A	0.00
	38%	Standard	3.99	0.99	N/A	N/A	4.20
	70%	Standard	1.99	0.86	3.96	0.15	43.04
	N/A	KU/KOLL Units	N/A	N/A	N/A	N/A	8.02
	N/A	Free - Promotion	3.97	0.99	0.00	N/A	0.00
	70%	Standard	4.97	1.94	4.97	0.29	22.93
	N/A	KU/KOLL Units	N/A	N/A	N/A	N/A	1.34

I have recently noticed that the number of borrows for each book has significantly increased. The total number of sales is now almost the same as the number of borrows. What I don't understand is why

Amazon is giving readers the opportunity to borrow an *unlimited* number of books. Some folks could easily take advantage of this in the countries where KU is available. An author can easily subscribe to KU and create a group of other authors who have books and are also subscribed to KU.

All of them pay $9.99 and they borrow each other's books. If the group has 100 authors and you borrow 1 book from all the authors, you basically pay them with $125-150 and you pay $9.99 for that. If all of them exchanged with you, you could win over $110. Who suffers? Amazon. I think they should restrict KU or increase the subscription price.

What's essential is that if someone borrows your book, he/she needs to read at least 10% of your book before you get paid for it. If this does not happen, you will not get any royalties.

For some readers, Kindle Unlimited is a good and cheap option. If someone reads a book every 2-3 days while travelling via subway or by any other public transport, he/she should spend $5 on average for one book. If he/she would read 3 books per week, that means 3 x $5 x 4 = $60/month or $720/year.

With Kindle Unlimited, he/she pays $9.99/month or $119.88/year and can read unlimited books. However, popular authors who have long series of books do not offer their books through KU and if you want to read it, you need to purchase it, even if you signed with KU.

Overall, KU is an excellent offer from Amazon both for readers and authors and it is constantly growing. KU has recently been made available for Canada, Australia, and Mexico, and it's also available for the US, UK, Germany, France, Spain, Italy, and Japan.

I highly recommend that all publishers enroll in KDP Select to take advantage of KU and the other tools offered by Amazon.

Note - When you sign up for KDP Select, you will automatically allow lending for your book. If you want to cancel this in the future to replace your borrows with sales, quit KDP Select and then make sure to upload the book on other platforms, too.

Chapter 12: Uploading Your Book

As soon as you finish writing your content, you have proofread your work, and you have a cover ready for your book, you can start uploading your book.

Step 1 – Go to http://kpd.amazon.com and go to "Bookshelf".

New Title Checklist:

✛
Create
new title

🔘 **Book Content:** You will be asked to upload your manuscript in a recommended format. We recommend using Kindle content creation tools to create children's books, educational content, comics and manga.

🔘 **Book Cover:** Use our online Cover Creator, or upload your cover in a supported format

🔘 **Description, Keywords and Categories:** Tell readers about your book and help them find it on Amazon

See all Getting Started tips ›

Step 2 – Enroll in KDP Select.

☐ **Enroll this book in KDP Select**

By checking this box, you are enrolling in KDP Select for 90 days. Books enrolled in KDP Select must not be available in digital format on any other platform during their enrollment. If your book is found to be available elsewhere in digital format, it may not be eligible to remain in the program. See the KDP Select Terms and Conditions and KDP Select FAQs for more information.

Step 3 – Enter Title, Subtitle, Book Series, and Description.

Step 4 – Add book contributors (click on "Author"). Make sure you don't choose "Editor" or anything else by mistake because they will tell you that you don't hold rights to the book (you're not the author) and they will terminate your account and you will have to explain to them that there was a mistake.

Step 5 – Choose "This is not a public domain work" as the book is your own work and no one will find it online for free.

2. Verify Your Publishing Rights

Verify Your Publishing Rights (What's this?)
- ○ This is a public domain work.
- ○ This is not a public domain work and I hold the necessary publishing rights.

Step 6 – Choose categories. Make sure to choose the best that fit your book. If you write erotica, set the minimum age to 18.

Step 7 – Keywords. Make sure that you have done the market research and you have chosen the best keywords. They have an enormous influence on your future sales and ranking.

Search keywords (up to 7, optional) (What's this?)

7 keywords left

Step 8 – Upload cover. Use JPEG or TIFF formats for covers.

Step 9 – Upload your content. Wait a few moments to upload.

Step 10 – Go to the next page, choose "Worldwide rights" or choose individual rights if you don't want to sell a book in some countries.

Step 11 – Choose your royalty 35% or 70%. If you price your book from $2.99 to $9.99, you will get 70% and if you price the book outside the 70% royalty, from $0.99 to $200 (maximum price), you will get 35%. At the beginning, price your book at $0.99.

Step 12 – Click on "Allow Lending" and make sure you have enrolled in KDP Select. This way, you can lend your book (you will make borrows).

Step 13 (Optional) – If you have a CreateSpace version, send Amazon an email to link the books on one page. Also tell them to update the number of pages from the paperback version to the Kindle version. It will appear "Contains real pages based on ISBN".

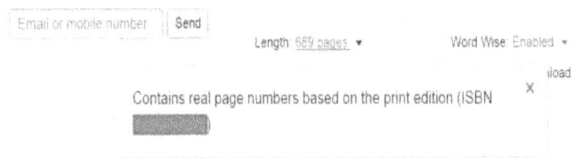

Step 13 (Optional) – Add your Audible ACX version to increase your sales even more.

Chapter 13: Outsourcing

If you don't have enough money to hire freelancers to do some basic tasks for you in the beginning, do it yourself. Once you start seeing money rolling in, try to outsource the time-consuming tasks to increase productivity. When you have dozens of books, you won't have enough time to manage all of them. You need to write, design covers, proofread your work, edit the book, format the book, come up with new ideas, do keyword research, ask friends and family for a couple of reviews, promote your book on websites, improve other old books, and so on. There are many tasks and things to take care of. So what are you going to do? At some point, you will get so tired of everything that you will quit or at least pause.

To avoid such things, you need to outsource these tasks. They are not expensive, but they are consuming your time.

Hire freelancers for:

- Proofreading
- Editing
- Creating a cover
- Rewriting an article/chapter
- Writing articles
- Promoting on websites

Proofreading and Editing – You can pay a freelancer to proofread and edit your work for $5/1,000 words (professional), $5/2,500 words or even $5/5,000 words on http://Fiverr.com. If your book has 20,000 words, you can have your book proofread and edited for as low as $20. To be sure that they are doing a good job, you can give your work to 2 proofreaders (not at the same time) for the best performance.

Creating a professional cover – You can have a cover created for $5 on http://Fiverr.com. Of course, high-quality covers can cost up to $100. I don't know how much money you make, or that you will make, but I think your time is more valuable than $5 (especially if you don't know anything about Photoshop or photo editing).

Rewrite chapters and articles – You can use http://iWriter.com for services from $3 up to $55 an article (ultimate quality).

Promote on websites – hire a VA on http://freelancer.com or http://odesk.com and you will pay him $2-3/hour to promote your book on websites and Facebook groups.

Chapter 14: Launching a New Kindle Book

Launching an eBook on Kindle is a complex task. It's a lot harder than you could ever imagine. Using a proper launching method could boost your book into the rankings and it can even make you a bestseller. You will probably ask yourself how that can be done. The process goes like this:

1. *KDP Select* - Make sure that you are enrolled in KDP Select to take advantage of the free promotional days in which you can promote your book 5 days every 90 days.

2. *Cover* - Design a professional cover. Do it yourself if you think you are capable (using Adobe Photoshop or another similar software). The cover is the first thing that interacts directly with your potential customers. A poor cover will make people avoid clicking on it. They will probably buy your book if it's the only one in a narrow niche, but this rarely happens.

If you don't have the necessary skills to create a professional cover, hire a freelancer to do it for you. Outsource this task. You have multiple options to choose from:

Http://odesk.com

Http://freelancer.com

Http://elance.com

Http://fiverr.com

Http://99designs.com

The most expensive covers will be on 99designs, but the quality will be the best, too. You can choose from 40-60 designs (you create a contest and you pick the winner) and this will cost you from $300 to $1,000.

The cheapest solution is to go on Fiverr and get it done for $5 (the cheapest solution). There are many Fiverr sellers who create eBook covers, and some of them are certified professionals. On Fiverr, you can have your cover done from $5 to $100. For $100, you will get a "Mastergig" for which you get the PDS File, unlimited revisions/modifications, the ability to choose from a variety of stock photos with license, and the work will be done 100% professionally.

I usually pay $20 for a cover that is also ready for publishing on CreateSpace (there are other requirements here) and I get a nice cover done within 3 days. To take advantage of this, go to http://Fiverr.com and type

"CreateSpace cover". You will find multiple Fiverr sellers who do an excellent job. As a tip, always contact a seller from Fiverr before purchasing anything.

3. Reviews - If you want to get many sales in the future, you will need reviews. When a customer sees your book, he/she looks at the cover, title, and reviews before he/she clicks on it to see more details. I do not encourage you to acquire fake reviews, I encourage you only to ask some friends and family to acquire 5-10 reviews before you start promoting a book. I have tested this on my own. A book with 0 reviews that I have recently released had 40 free downloads, while the same book with 10 reviews got me over 150 free downloads (without any additional promotions or paid services).

You will get reviews from the people who take your book for free. The conversion goes like this: 1 to 3 reviews for every 1,000 free units. For paid units, 1% of your customers will write a review for you, so for each 100 units you sell, 1 or possibly 2 people will take the time to write a review. It's sad but most customers from Kindle leave reviews if 1.) they are really satisfied with it and they leave a 5-star review or 2.) they are really pissed off and they give you a 1-star review (or 2 stars). You will rarely receive 3-star reviews.

The more reviews you get, the higher you rank in Amazon's algorithm. There are 3 ways to get more reviews (naturally):

- Use email lists and ask your readers to typely leave a review (Explain to them how essential it is for you).

- Ask your family and friends to have a look at your book.

- Promote your book in as many places as you can (Udemy announcements, YouTube comments, free websites, paid promotions (websites, tweets, Facebook groups).

4. Free downloads - Amazon allows you to promote your book for 5 days every 90 days (KDP Select Program) and the mechanism is simple: the more free downloads you make, the more money you will make after the promotion. Amazon will promote your book if people are interested in buying it and it will also rank your book high in the searches. From my experience, I have noticed that a book that gets over 2,000 downloads sells really well after the promotion (if it's high quality, of course). The conversion rate for free downloads is for every 100 free units, you will get around 1 sale in the following 1-2 days.

5. *Advertising* - To acquire over 2,000 downloads you will need to put forth a lot of effort. You won't make more than 200 free units if you just give away the book for free and do nothing. You will need to submit it to a free website, Kindle groups (readers), use an email list, use advanced marketing techniques, pay for promotional services, and you will make over 2,000 units. If you want from 1,000 to 3,000 units, you need to do the following:

- Join Facebook groups.

- Create a Pinterest account and submit it there.

- Create an Udemy account and join free courses about Kindle Publishing, Amazon,

Amazon tricks, etc. (any course that involves Amazon)

- Go on YouTube and leave comments on videos about Kindle Publishing, Amazon etc.

- Look for free websites to submit your book. There are over 100! Just type "free website to promote Kindle books" on Google and you will find dozens of websites.

- Go on Fiverr.com and give your book to some Fiverr sellers to promote it. You will have your book submitted to over 60 Facebook Groups of readers for $5.

- Buy a few services at $10 (I will include a list).

Using these, you will pay around $25 and get somewhere between 1,000 and 3,000 free downloads, which is really good. If you want to dominate the market and to invest accordingly into professional services, take the following into consideration:

- Go to http://freebooksy.com and submit your book. You will need to pay $80 for nonfiction or $100 for fiction and you will get between 2,000 and 6,000 free downloads (it depends on the niche, cover, reviews, length, etc.).

- Go to http://bookbub.com and submit your book. There is a huge pricing list and they also estimate the number of downloads that you will get. For $240, you will get from 8,000 to 27,000 free downloads. You must have a good quality book, over 100 pages, good reviews, and a decent cover. Before they promote your book, they will check it professionally (to be well formatted, to have no grammar errors, etc. If your book passes their test, you have an excellent book.

- Go on http://Fiverr.com and invest $30 in different gigs. They will promote on Facebook, Twitter, websites, and blogs. (expect 500 - 1,000 free downloads).

- Do everything I have mentioned for the 1,000 - 3,000 downloads section.

- Snowball effect. As soon as your book gets over 5,000 downloads, it will be listed in the top #100 free books on Amazon and people will see your book and you will get a lot more new downloads thanks to the excellent exposure that you have.

Using all of these methods, you will easily exceed 30,000 downloads and you will invest $350 in total. You will probably ask yourself if it's worth it. It is, but it will depend on the quality of your book, the number of reviews, the topic, and the length of the book. You will get your money back in approximately 1 or 2 months (again, it depends on the price point, cover, content, etc.). If you are lucky enough, you can get your money back in less than a week. *Note – There is nothing wrong or immoral in paying for advertising. All of the world's manufacturers, producers, and artists invest in advertising, ads, etc. This is basically a method that Amazon encourages through KDP Select. There is nothing wrong with submitting your book to a list or a group of **real** readers who will click to download/purchase your book if they are interested in it. What is immoral, dishonest, and unforgivable is to pay for services that use bots or programs to create fake accounts and make you fake downloads to artificially inflate your ranking. If you ever see on some "books" in the Top #100 free books section that have 15-20 pages with no reviews, have been published 2 days earlier, and are ranked #10 or #20 or even less in the WHOLE*

Kindle store... well... those are manipulators, cheaters, hackers, or whatever you want to call them.

6. Price - Make sure to price your book high during the promotion and to drop down the price to $0.99 before the promotion ends, so you can make a lot of purchases right after to increase your overall paid rank. It's quite obvious – if you would get a free book that was $0.99 and you can also get a free book that was $5.99, which one would you get? You receive a higher "value" from the $5.99 book because the discount offered is bigger. This encourages more people to download your book during the promotion.

Soon after the promotion ends, your book will start getting purchases at $0.99, and, of course, the number of purchases will depend on the number of free downloads that you had during the free promotion. The free promotion will provide visibility and a powerful boost in sales.

I recommend to price the book at $0.99 for 3 days after the promotion and then price it at $2.99 or $3.99 (you choose the final price). Also, the price of the book is essential for keeping your rank high enough.

There are 2 methods that you can choose from:

1.) You price your book at $2.99 after all the promotions and you leave it that way. By doing this, people will buy your book for multiple reasons - because looks good, because they are interested in the topic, because it's cheap, or just because they are curious in buying something new. The $2.99 price is also a plus against others who have a book similar to yours but is priced at $3.99 or more. Also, if your book has 140 pages and it's $2.99, and other authors have a book with 50 pages and it's also $2.99, it will be more likely for customers to buy your book.

2.) Price your book at $3.99 or more. There is another group of people who prefer to pay more for quality. When they see $2.99, they may think, *This book is crap if it's only 3 bucks*. So, by pricing the book at $4.99, it will change some people's way of thinking and judging.

My advice

I prefer 1.) because you make more sales and you keep your rank high. If you sell 10 copies at $2.99, you are ranked somewhere at #15,000 - #20,000 and you have pretty good chances of becoming a bestseller also. If you sell your book at $4.99, you get $3.00 royalty and if you sell 5 each day instead of 10, your rank will be around #40,000-#50,000. That rank won't make you a bestseller. Basically, for $2.99 you make $2.97 x 10 = $20 and for $4.99, you make $3.00 x 5 = $17. This is just an example, I may be wrong, but usually, sales go up when the prices go down. The main advantage here is that you increase your rank and keep it high. Using all these methods will successfully launch your book and make it a bestseller (depending on the topic of your book).

Note - Avoid using services such as "Freebookservice". They use bots to download your book from 1 IP address and Amazon will see that immediately and they can terminate your KDP account without contacting you (they usually contact you). Amazon does not complain about promoting your book to groups of readers.

That's what you basically do, even when you pay on websites. They promote your book on different platforms, email lists, websites, blogs, and groups in exchange for a commission (you pay the commission). It's absolutely legal and moral to do that, but it's absolutely immoral to promote a book by "hacking" Amazon's algorithm with bots and fake accounts.

Chapter 15: Ranking

Every single author wants to be successful in his own way and with his own books. To become successful, sell many books, and generate an impressive amount of money, you need to rank your books really high.

#1 Best Seller

The mechanism is simple. Amazon uses its own Search Engine Optimization algorithm, which ranks your book depending on several factors. However, the most essential factor is the number of sales you are able to generate each day. Amazon updates the ranks hourly and it compares your sales with other authors' sales and based on this, it ranks your book.

As a small rank guide, here are some numbers:

#200,000 - 1,000,000 for 0 sales/day (your book is forgotten, outranked by others)

#100,000 - 200,000 for 1 sale every 2 days (weak, easy to get outranked)

#70,000 - 99,000 for 1 sale/day (entry level)

#50,000 - 69,000 for 2-3 sales/day (not bad, you are making $150/month with one title)

#30,000 - 49,000 for 4-5 sales/day (decent)

#20,000 - 29,000 for 6-7 sales/day (good, you will become a bestseller for narrow subcategories)

#10,000 – 19,000 for 8-10 sales/day (wonderful, you're making over $500/month)

#5,000 - 10,000 for 10-15 sales/day (excellent, you're a bestseller for at least 1 category)

#3,000 – 5,000 for 15-20 sales/day (100% bestseller)

#1,000 – 3,000 for 20-50 sales/day (congratulations!)

#500 – 1,000 for 50-200 sales/day (wow!)

#250-500 for 200-500 sales/day (speechless!)

#100-250 for 500-1,000 sales/day (!!)

#under 100 for 1,000-2,000 sales/day (mind blowing!)

#1 - over 5,000 sales/day (insane)

Note - Your rank will increase even if a customer borrows a book. If you sell 2 books and all the other authors sell 3, your rank will drop. If no one sells any books, your rank remains the same or even increases. Rankings are per store - this means that for the US store, you have a rank, for the UK store, a different rank, etc. You may have #20,000 rank in US, #100,000 in UK, and #8,000 in Canada and India. Generally, the biggest stores are US, UK, CA, AU, IN (descending order, with the US being the biggest) and then the others.

What you want to achieve with any book you have is to become a bestseller for any category. For instance, you may become a bestseller for a narrow category if you are ranked at #40,000, which means that you make 3-4 sales a day.

Besides sales, there are other methods that you need to apply for ranking. In fact, there are 2 types of ranking in Amazon: your paid rank (or free) and the rank for keywords (like Google's algorithms).

To rank high in Amazon's searches, you need:

1. Optimized keywords
2. Reviews (preferably verified reviews)
3. Sales

Chapter 16: Perma-free books

One of the best marketing strategies that you can use to exponentially increase your sales for all your books is to create a perma-free book. Perma-free books are books that are permanently free on Amazon or any other platform, and, believe it or not, most of professional publishers have at least one or two. A perma-free book should be created as a start for a series, and it's the best way to attract new readers and subscribers. The mechanism behind this is simple - if someone downloads your free book and likes it, that person will definitely take a look at all your other books to see what he/she would like to buy from you.

Even if that person does want to buy anything for you but follows you, then your number of free downloads will increase for each promotion, and in the end, those will convert into sales. A perma-free book will usually get 50-150 downloads every day. From those 100 downloads (on average), at least 10 people will follow you or will buy something from you. To take advantage of this, you can also upload a perma-free book on Nook, Smashwords, and other similar platforms. Of course, to direct your readers from a place to another, you will need to include some links to your other books on Amazon.

How to set up a perma-free book

Step 1 - Publish the book at $0.99 on Amazon and *do not* enroll in KDP Select.
Step 2 - Publish the book on Nook or another platform and set it for free.
Step 3 - Send Amazon Support an email in which you tell them that your book is already on Nook or another platform for free and you want it to make it free on Kindle.
As soon as you publish the free book on Nook or another platform for free, make

sure to announce Amazon by clicking on the link. (See photo)

Amazon Best Sellers Rank: #63,703 Paid in Kindle Store (See Top 100 Paid in Kindle Store)

#43 in Kindle Store > Kindle eBooks > Business & Money > Marketing & Sales > **Advertising**

#57 in Kindle Store > Kindle eBooks > Business & Money > **Accounting**

#58 in Kindle Store > Kindle eBooks > Business & Money > Marketing & Sales > Marketing > **Web Marketing**

Would you like to **give feedback on images** or **tell us about a lower price?**

Note - Use a perma-free book for every 10-15 books that you have in series. By creating a series of books, you will engage your readers to follow you and to make them want to learn more from you.

Chapter 17: Keywords

Behind the success of every book is marketing and optimization, which can be done using several techniques. I will discuss the importance of keywords and how to choose the best keywords for your books. There are books on Amazon that have excellent content and excellent reviews, but they don't sell really well because they don't have the right keywords. If you manage to choose the best keywords for your books, you will obtain amazing profits.

First of all, for every book you publish, you are allowed to use up to 7 keywords, so all you have to do is to find the best keywords on Amazon and Google. Secondly, you can include some keywords in your description, title, subtitle, and series (the name of the series). The more keywords you have, the more exposure you will get.

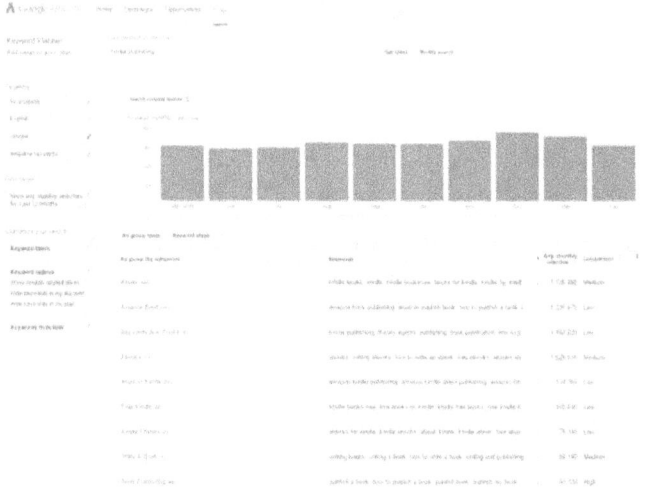

Step 1 - Use Amazon's search bar and look for suggestions. Example, for the keyword "How to", Amazon will give you some suggestions based on the number of searches on the website. They will appear in descending order of the number of searches/results.

Step 2 - Go to Google.com and type "keyword planner". Google AdWords will appear at the top. Click on it and create an account. Next, go to "keyword planner", type a broad keyword (examples - love, publishing, how to, etc., and click on "Get Ideas". You will immediately see results from Google with detailed information - number of monthly searches, competition, average bid, and others.

Step 3 - Make a correlation between Amazon's keywords and Google's keywords.

Step 4 - Look on Amazon for books that have those keywords and study the market. Look for books that are selling well, that have good reviews, and track them. Use them as a model for your future book, but use the best keywords you find.

Step 5 - Use your keywords when you publish your book.

Tips

1. *Keyword density (text ratio)* - When you use a keyword, study the text ratio before publishing your book. Example - the keyword "motivational quotes", which

appears in the context "Motivational quotes for getting things done" has a text ratio of 33% (2 out of 6 words represent the keyword). If you put just "Motivational quotes", you have a text ratio of 100%. If you put "Motivational quotes for getting things done as fast as possible and achieving success" has 15%. The bigger your text ratio is, the higher you rank for that specific keyword.

2. *Reviews -* If you have a book with 50 reviews and your competitor has 45 reviews, your book will rank higher. If your book has 50 reviews that include the keyword and your competitor has 50 reviews without the keyword, you will rank higher than him.

3. *Description and Title* - Make sure to include your keywords in your description and title to rank even higher.

4. **Broad Keywords** - Use broad keywords and promote your book (get thousands of free downloads) for the best results.

Chapter 18: CreateSpace

Even if Kindle stands for digital books and most of the customers buy Kindle books, there are a few people who prefer to read a physical book. To please all your customers, you can create a paperback version for your Kindle books and this will help you increase your profits.

Generally, for every 5 Kindle books that you sell, you will also sell a physical one so you will increase your profits by around 20% (overall).

How much does it cost?

It's free to get started, but if you want to, you can invest in using their services for proofreading and for the cover. I honestly don't recommend you to use their services because they are really expensive and not worth the price. I generally use Fiverr and pay $10 to $20 for a good looking cover and for that price, you get the 2D flat cover for Kindle and the PDF format for CreateSpace.

CreateSpace will assign a free ISBN for your book or you can use your own if you have any. The uploading process is really simple. You only need to complete some fields and then send the book to approval, which will take around 12 to 24 hours. Once approved, it will be available on Amazon within 3 business days.

‣ See all 2 formats and editions

Kindle	Paperback
$1.23	$7.99
Read with our free app	5 New from $7.99

Note - Email them and tell them to link your book to the Kindle version so it will appear in 2 formats on the same page. They say that this will happen automatically, but for me, it never did, I always had to tell them to link them manually.

Trim Sizes

This is a very tricky aspect that many authors and publishers are not aware of. In fact, I didn't know either until I did some experiments and saw it for myself.

Kindle books without any print versions always have their page estimation based on A4 format, which is insanely big. A real book will never have that size unless it's a 2,000 page encyclopedia.

The most common trim sizes are 5 x 8 inches and 6 x 9 inches. When I surf Amazon, I often see books that have 27 - 40 books that can be bought in a paperback format and have a 6 x 9 size. Is that a joke? A 6 x 9 book with 30 pages (table of contents, introduction, and conclusion have 5 pages)? That book has a thickness of 0. 5 inches. It's ridiculous.

For books that have less than 200-220 pages, I use the 5 x 8 format. You have many advantages by using this format -

you get more pages and engage readers, the book is compact and easy to carry, it's easier to hold it in the hand, and it makes it easier to read. It literally looks professional. If you think that this size is small, take a ruler and measure 5 inches width and 8 inches height. I think you will find it big enough.

I use the 6 x 9 for books that have over 250 pages, because the spine will get too thick and it will deteriorate faster and it will be harder to open it; it will become annoying.

From 100 pages in A4, you will obtain around 150 pages in 6 x 9 format and around 180 pages in 5 x 8 format (font size has a big influence). When you see books with no paperback versions that have 70-80 pages, those books are more than 130 pages in reality. This is not a scam to make people think that they pay for more pages, but Amazon's approximations are false.

Process:

1. Go to http://CreateSpace.com and sign up with them. Complete the tax interview (the same as for KDP).

2. Choose Payment Method (Direct Deposit or Check)

3. Go to "Member Dashboard". Click on "Add new title". Put in your title, choose "Paperback", and choose one of the two methods "Guided" or "Expert". By doing in Expert mode, you will finish faster, but you need to be familiar with the whole process. If it's your first time, choose "Guided".

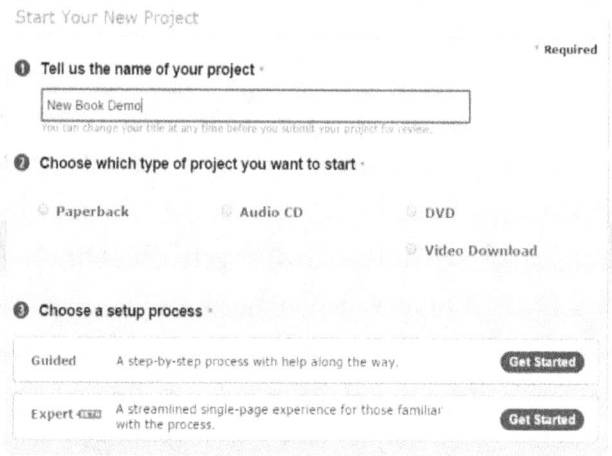

Start Your New Project

❶ Tell us the name of your project *

New Book Demo|

You can change your title at any time before you submit your project for review.

❷ Choose which type of project you want to start *

○ Paperback   ○ Audio CD   ○ DVD

○ Video Download

❸ Choose a setup process *

| Guided | A step-by-step process with help along the way. | Get Started |
| Expert ⬛ | A streamlined single-page experience for those familiar with the process. | Get Started |

4. Assign a free CreateSpace ISBN and click continue. Add your author name (or pen name).

5. Upload a cover (PDF format). Upload the interior (DOC file for Guided, PDF for Expert – to save a DOC file as PDF, click on Save As – PDF format).

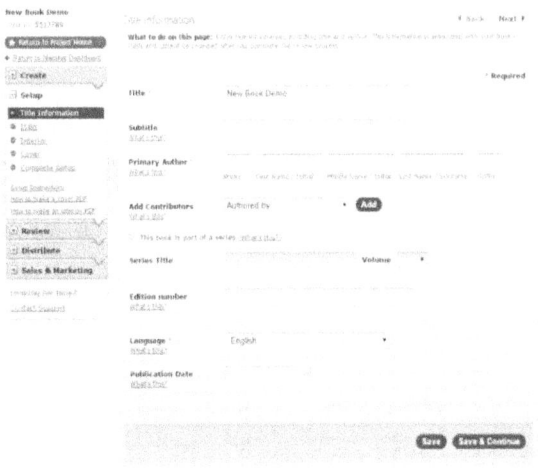

6.   Price your book. Choose the trim size (I use 5 x 8 or 6 x 9). Choose paper type – cream or white. Choose paper color – Black & White or Full-Color (Full color are expensive to print and you need to price them over $11.99 so don't do it unless you have a long book with photos).

7.   Choose Keywords (up to 5).

8.   Choose category. Submit Files for review. Wait 24 hours for them to respond and approve your book. Proof your book (enter the Digital Proofreader, take a look at your book, and then exit and click "Approve").

Once approved, your book is live. Once your book appears live in paperback format, make sure to enroll in Kindle Matchbook – people who buy the paperback format will receive the Kindle version for free or for a low fee – $0.99 - $1.99.

kindle matchbook

Chapter 19: Reviews

Verified Reviews

When a person downloads your book for free or purchases it, if they write a review, it will appear as a "Verified Purchase". This type of reviews are powerful for increasing the rank and visibility of a book and also gives authority to the review. Each Verified Review will look like this:

Without a doubt, you will get negative reviews. I did, so did Tony Robbins, and so does everyone. The negative reviews don't reflect the reality all the time, some people will give you a 1-star rating without commenting why because they are jealous or hate you because of your success.

Unverified Reviews

Unverified reviews can be given by any "Guest" who sees your book. These reviews come from people who borrow your book or who like/don't like its first appearance of if they spotted something wrong in the title or description.

Negative Reviews

Even if someone borrows your book (it isn't a verified purchase), they can review your book. What annoys me is that your competitors can easily click on your book and write a negative review (unverified) without even looking at your book and without buying it. You can't avoid them, they just happen. To overcome negative reviews, you should try to get in touch with your customers and tell them that you are sorry for the inconvenience, give them another copy of another book, or update what bothers them to the book that they have purchased. Tell them that you are sorry and ask them to change the review because it is essential for you.

You can also vote "No" for the review and it will drop down. If the negative review reflects the reality, other customers who experienced the same will vote "Yes" for that review and it will go up and be visible for everyone. Some negative reviews reflect reality and will tell you where you made mistakes. Try to take them as a warning, and improve your book to avoid getting other similar negative reviews. Generally, if your book is high quality, you will get very few negative reviews, but you will get some anyway. There is no such thing as "the perfect book". *Note – Amazon pays serious attention to books that have a 5 /5 rating and checks the reviews. After all, I have never a seen a book with 500 reviews all of 5 stars, that's impossible. Every single author from Kindle has negative reviews.*

Chapter 20: Pen Names

When you write a book, you do not have to use your real name, and I advise you not to for some obvious reasons. A pen name is the name under which you write. I have also used some pen names myself, but I prefer to keep them private.

Mark Twain is a pen name. If you search on Google, you will find out his real name, too. Singers, performers, magicians, and writers use pen names or stage names. If you are using a pen name, it doesn't mean that you are hiding from people or you are ashamed of who you really are.

If you start a new publishing business and you want to write about business, but you are also passionate about gardening and cooking, it won't go well of you write books about cooking, recipes, business, and gardening. It will confuse people. Use a pen name for gardening, one for business, and one for cooking.

If you write a book for the first time, use a pen name. You will make mistakes as a beginner and you have to constantly improve yourself. Let's say you wrote 5 books and you made mistakes and you even got some negative reviews. Do you think that someone will buy your 6th book? I don't think so.

Even Amazon encourages you to use a pen name in their guidelines and they even allow you to sign up for Author Central and you can have up to 3 pen names on one account.

Sign up with Author Central to track your author rank, book ranks, followers, and increase your sales. People generally want to know who the author is before making a purchase. If you have more than 3 pen names, make sure to put the best ones you have.

To sign up with Author Central, go to the following link:

https://authorcentral.amazon.com

Chapter 21: Bundles

One effective strategy to sell more books and to attract more potential customers and subscribers is to create bundles from your existing books. I like to create bundles out of a small series of books that have something in common (one bundle is on its way, stay tuned).

For example, if you have a book about Kindle publishing, one about Kindle publishing tips, and one about book marketing, you can make a bundle out of them. The general price of these are 3 at the price of 2 or somewhere around - 50%. If you have 3 books about a related topic (a series) and they have over 100 pages each, and they are $2.99, you can create a bundle of over 300 pages priced at $4.99. It's really effective and profitable, you basically increase your income from these three books by up to 20%.

If you are selling 4-5 units a day for each topic at $2.99, you are selling approximately 15 units a day, which is almost $31. By putting out a bundle, if you sell at least 1 every day, that is another $3 a day. That is more than 10% more, but remember that you can do better than that. A book with 300 pages, with good quality content, and priced at $4.99, is a complete bargain.

I've seen many successful authors who are applying this strategy, especially those who are selling erotica books. At every 2-3 books, they make a bundle, at every 5 books, a different bundle, and at 10 books, a master-bundle.

Note - 1 bundle for every 5 books that you have (for a series) is an efficient way to boost your sales.

Chapter 22: Writing Plan

One of the most essential things that you want to take into consideration is to make an organized writing plan. Schedule all your tasks, spread them into days, weeks, and months before getting started.

If you do not make a plan for yourself, you will never know where to start and you will get confused and not be productive at all.

My plan:

Find a good topic to write about.

1. Plan your book title and the chapters. Write down the ideas you have and make sure to add enough chapters to cover a full-length book.

Write 1,000 – 3,000 words every day. In fact, write as little as you want, but don't let a single day pass without putting down a few words. Even if you feel tired or you feel that you don't feel inspired to write about a topic, write something just short of 500 words. When you wake up the next day, new ideas will come up and will fill in the gaps. The best tip for a writer is to never stop writing. Writing 1,000–3,000 words every day won't take you more than 2 hours.

2. Do additional research – Look on Amazon, and download materials that you might need for your books and analyze them.

   Schedule promotions (if you have many books) and note down every schedule you make. Set reminders for them. Don't forget that you can promote your book 5 or 7 days every 90 days, and use them wisely. Hire other people to design a cover, promote your book, or to give you some ideas for your book. You can even hire a ghost writer to write some content for you.

Outsource tasks and focus on your own – promotions, good quality content.

3. Make deadlines for finishing your books – This will maximize your productivity if you always keep in mind that you have to work and you have to finish something until a fixed date. After you finish your work, take some time for yourself, relax, and enjoy the rest of the day.

I usually publish a book every month and I don't rush. I like to take my time and do excellent work. You will see many crappy books from unknown authors on Kindle. I am not that type of author and I hope you won't be either. What I am encouraging you here is to create good quality books and to create a successful publishing business.

As soon as I finish my book (in approximately 2 weeks), I send my work to 1 or 2 proofreaders and I wait another week to be ready. While it's being proofread, I do serious research for the keywords I will use for my book. As soon as I have finished choosing the right keywords (which takes less than a day), I order a cover that will be done in 2-3 days. I upload my book on Kindle, I upload my book on CreateSpace, I tell them to link the versions, and then I start to promote it. I submit my book to as many free websites as possible, as well as on some paid websites.

Whenever I have new ideas, or I think of something and an idea pops up in my head, I quickly note it down. It doesn't matter where you are; you have your smartphone, laptop, tablet, whatever. Just note down your ideas.

I use Evernote for putting down my ideas. It's basically a cloud for notes, notebooks, stacks of notebooks, and it has many, many more applications. The basic version is free and it's limited.

You can use Evernote simultaneously on Android, iOS, Mac OS, or Windows and it syncs instantly. It's really an excellent piece of software and you can even set reminders for every note you take. It's one of the best productivity apps you can use. I will cover more about software and resources in a separate chapter.

Chapter 23: Maintenance

As you may know, Kindle publishing is a unique way of making money online, a passive income stream. I have heard many people say "Autopilot", "you will set up several books and you're done", or "once you upload them, they will bring you money month after month without doing anything else".

WRONG.

Passive income is a way to generate money...passively, but there is no such thing as 100% Passive Income. You have to promote, write, hire others, come up with new ideas, etc. If you don't believe it, upload 5 books and leave them there for 1 year and see what happens. The truth is that these books need maintenance from time to time, not every week or every month, but they do need attention. It isn't a heavy task to maintain a book, but when you have 50 books, if you want to make money out of them, you will need to take care of them.

How to maintain your books

The first thing that you have to do is to promote your books again every 90 days, as you are allowed to promote your books 5 days every 90 days using Free days or 7 days every 90 days using Countdown deals. If you forget to use your days, you won't receive any more, so I highly recommend you to use reminders for when to promote your books again.

Each time you promote a book again, use websites and paid services to boost rankings. I have already said that, but what I want to underline is that promoting a book once won't be enough to maintain it high in the rankings for a year. You need to permanently promote it and also try to use new services. The ones you used in the beginning won't give you the best results when you use them again. Occasionally (once a year), you should change the cover of the book. It has a huge impact on people. Also, you should have a look at your book and try to add something new to it. After that, write in the description or even in the new cover, something like "Updated 2015". It will help you maintain your ranking over years. Permanently release new books and mention one of your books or all of them at the end of each new book. Customers who like your book will be curious to see your work.

Changing keywords is another way to shift to another audience (in case the book starts to drop in rankings). If you are selling well, don't do this – promoting it for free or for a countdown deal is more than enough (again, if the book is selling good).

No matter how good a book is selling, paying for promotional services will always boost your ranking, so I advise you to take this into account. If your book is not doing great, schedule a free promotion and promote your book while it's free. If it's doing well, drop the price to $0.99 and pay for services that promote books at $0.99. I will include all the resources you need in the "Resources" chapter.

Chapter 24: Becoming an Authority

Many authors are known on Amazon based on the category of eBooks that they're selling in.

Becoming a "local" authority on Kindle isn't easy, but it's surely profitable if you work hard and focus on your tasks.

To become an authority in front of other authors, you need:

1. Hundreds of reviews
2. As many books as possible
3. To release a book every month
4. To promote your books all the time
5. To improve your books all the time
6. To occasionally change covers
7. To get informed all the time
8. To offer bonuses to readers

9. To make your readers like you and follow you
10. To create good quality content

The best way to promote your books is to release other new books. By using this theory, you are on your way to ultimate success.

When your books reach over 100-200 reviews, you will dominate the niche that you are in (at least 90% of it), you will outrank others, and you will become a true authority. That big number of reviews will rank you high enough in almost any related search very easily. To acquire that number of reviews isn't easy – you need to permanently improve your books and to be sure that they are excellent quality and promote them all the time – forums, blogs, on your blog, on YouTube (make a book intro), iun Facebook groups (of readers), Twitter, free websites, paid websites, paid promotions, etc.

When you release a book every month, you will reach new readers for that topic. If the readers like your work, they will surely have a look at your other books. In other words, by releasing a new book, you will passively increase the sales of your other books. The more books you have, the better the others will sell.

Of course, this strategy is a long-term one and it needs a lot of work and concentration. It's not easy, but it's not impossible.

Chapter 25: The Six-Figure Autopilot

If you would release a book with 150 pages each month, in 1 year, you would easily be making 12 books. If you add 2 or 3 bundles, you will reach 15 books. With 15 books, you can earn over $4,000/month if you follow this guide and these strategies. Not every book sells, but you will have 1 or 2 that will sell really good, 7-8 that sell okay, and probably a few that won't do really good.

If you manage to release 25-30 books in 2 years just by writing 1 book a month and promoting it (this includes investing money), you can easily exceed $10,000/month, which is $120,000/year.

You will have expenses, tax withhold rates, local taxes, and others, but you will manage to generate a gross income of at least $10,000 if you release 30 such books. Guaranteed.

2 years may sound like a long time, but imagine that some people are learning and going through university for years and when they graduate, they earn about $35,000/year. A CEO or a Senior Employee earns over $100,000 a year but it takes a lot of work for that person to be in that position.

Publishing good quality books isn't easy and it's competitive, but in the long-term, it's profitable. eBooks won't disappear. It's fast, efficient, eco-friendly, and you can store unlimited eBooks on one single device.

There are people on Amazon who earn over $1,000,000 a year and they are not smarter than you and me. They worked hard, they invested in their books, they had patience, and they have followed their instincts. The #1 Bestseller on Kindle sells overs 3,000 copies a day and the price isn't $2.99, it's around $6.99. Just think for a second – 3,000 x $6.99 x 0.0 royalty x 30 days = $441,000. If that book stays in the first place for 2 months, it generates over $1 million. In fact, that books generates more than $441,000.00 – all those books have Audible Narration, paperback versions, even hardcovers, which also sell over 100-200 copies a day. That book may sell more than 5,000 copies, it's number #1, it can sell 20,000 and no one can know exactly how many copies sell.

This is what I call... the power of Amazon.

Chapter 26: Setting Goals

Successful people, entrepreneurs, and life enthusiasts set goals for themselves to achieve what they dreamed of. To get the best results, to increase your productivity and to be motivated, you need to set short-term and long-term goals.

Short-term goals

- Your next book will have at least 20,000 words. You will make at least $500 a month from your new book.
- You will create at least 1 book per month.
- You will go on a vacation every two months.
- You will create 1 blog post every week.
- You will create a YouTube video every 2 weeks.

- You will save at least $250 each month.

The list goes on. Setting such goals will not only help you be more productive and motivated but it will also help you organize your life effectively.

Long-term goals

- Buy a car
- Save $100,000
- Create 20 books
- Become a millionaire
- Buy real estate properties

All these goals need some deadlines so they can have a positive effect on you. Maybe you will sometimes think that these dreams won't be realizable, but the truth is that the more you want and the more you dream of, the more you will achieve. Even if it won't be 100% of what you initially wanted, setting a big goal will help you run toward it and you will achieve at least 50-70% of it.

In the beginning, set some goals regarding time, money, tasks, and a number of books. I have already mentioned that it's efficient and profitable to release a book a month, but you can do even more than that.

I have my own goals and believe it or not, it really helps me. It helps me especially when I set a deadline to finish a book and I always say to myself, "I have to work today, I have to finish this today, I need to finish this by the end of the week." It pushes you from behind and it's very effective.

Just make a list with what you want to achieve and what you want for the next 3 months. Imagine yourself how would you like to be (financially) in 3 months and write down some goals. Also, make sure to respect them.

Chapter 27: Motivation

Setting goals requires motivation.

Motivation is hard to manage all the time, but once achieved, you are unstoppable. Every person has his own way of getting motivated, every person has his own dream and purpose in life, and every person sees life differently and lives differently. If you haven't found what motivates you, keep looking. You will find it.

Many of us would like to start a business, try something new, or discover new areas of life. There are some facts that influence people not to start their own business or to not follow their dreams.

- Fear - If you want to start your own business or try something, but you are scared, think that you have 2 options: your fears will hold you back or your fears will give you the momentum to face them.

- You don't want to fail - A life full of mistakes is more honorable than a life in which you haven't done anything. No one is perfect, but you have to keep improving yourself and learn from mistakes.
- It's too hard - Nothing in this world is easy. Whatever you do, it's hard, but try to pick something you enjoy and that is profitable at the same time.
- I don't have the skills – No one is born skilled. Skills can be learned and can be improved. All you have to do is to keep working.
- I don't have time - This is probably the most commonly used excuse of all. Whether you have a mediocre job or you are a millionaire, you have 24 hours. Everyone has 24 hours, so how do successful people manage to achieve success? They manage their time effectively. Instead of wasting your time with

useless things, make some time to develop yourself.

- I don't have the money - There are many things that you can start online (including Kindle publishing or starting a publishing business) that don't require money, or they require the lowest fees.
- I don't have good ideas - New ideas come on the go, so start as soon as possible.
- I can't do it until it's perfect - Nothing in this world is perfect. Launch your product, your book, even if it isn't perfect. Nothing is perfect, neither me nor you, nor anyone.
- BUT - This is probably the worst of all. BUT is a killer. You would start a business, but... You would like to, but... But what? Eliminate "but" from your vocabulary.

No pain, no gain - If you don't work hard enough, you won't achieve what you wish for. You need to sacrifice your time and your focus on more profitable things. Your own business needs to be the number one priority if you want to succeed. If you don't succeed in it, it means you don't want it that bad.

You need to believe in yourself, to be optimistic, and to always improve yourself. Everything is challenging, so challenge yourself.

Persistence is the only thing that you need to achieve *anything*.
*"Nothing in the world can take the place of persistence. Talent will not; nothing is more common than unsuccessful men with talent. Genius will not; unrewarded genius is almost a proverb. Education will not; the world is full of educated derelicts. Persistence and determination alone are omnipotent. The slogan 'Press On!' has solved and always will solve the problems of the human race." - **Calvin Coolidge**

Chapter 28: Creating the Backend of the Books

If you want to make a killing by selling books on Amazon, you have to do a lot of research and create an online empire (which includes Amazon). The backend of your books needs to be created if you want to create a real online business.

You need:

- A blog
- Digital courses
- A YouTube channel
- Social Media accounts
- A podcast
- An email list
- A Google AdSense account (for blog & YouTube)

Creating a blog will allow you to contact all your readers who liked your work. By writing quality books and by offering them at a low price point (even for free – perma-free books), you will attract new people to your blog, website, and you start building an email list. You

Create a course (free & paid) on Udemy or Shareaskill, or even on YouTube, with what you do and what you love. Share your experience with others and funnel them to your blog, courses, books, and everything you have.

Create an email list. To convince people to subscribe to your blog, you need to make sure that it's high quality and you give them something for free (a book, a course). Every successful website or blog has an email list for multiple purposes. In our case, you can use the email list to promote your books where they are discounted or free.

The Google AdSense account will be used for adding ads on your blog and on your YouTube channel. You won't make much money from it, but more than enough to cover your expenses for email marketing services ($19/month – Aweber – email services & auto responder), hosting, content you write, etc.

Podcast – Many successful publishers have their own podcast in which they present their books, their thoughts, they offer tips from their experience, or even some small parts of their books. This should be free for everyone, but you need to make this high quality (you will need a professional microphone) to engage them and make them follow you.

Create social media accounts and make people follow you – Create a Facebook page, accounts on Twitter, LinkedIn, Pinterest, Instagram, etc.

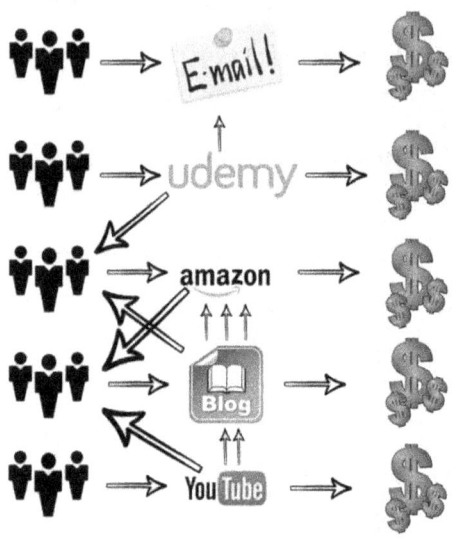

Create YouTube videos every 1-2 weeks with things that you love and that you also have in your books. By creating videos with yourself talking, this will provide credibility and authority in front of others. You don't have to be an online guru who hides behind a computer screen.

What should your backend look like?

At the end of the book, make a dedicated chapter or page with your blog and your free gift and add a text like "For more information on related topics, subscribe to my blog and get your free gift – an eBook about Online Marketing". On your blog, post links to the other stuff you have – courses, books, podcast, YouTube channel, social media accounts, etc.

The whole process is simple. The more people you reach, the more money you will make from all these platforms. This process requires a lot of time, money, and effort, but this is how successful online entrepreneurs create their own empire.

Chapter 29: Amazon Ad Campaigns

Amazon has recently released a campaign in which you can pay for ads based on the PPC (Pay Per Click) method. Amazon will place ads on different pages (they generally place your book on pages related to your topic) and whenever someone clicks on the ad, you will be charged.

The minimum amount required to start a campaign is $100 and the minimum PPC bid is $0. 2. You can set the bid from 0. 2 to $5 and the idea is simple: the more you pay for each bid, the higher the chances are to convert those clicks into sales.

You have a dedicated dashboard for managing ad campaigns. You can see the number views, impressions, clicks, and sales generated. The average conversion rates are 3 – 7%.

Example – For an average bid of $0. 5, you get 400 clicks. If you convert 5% of those into sales, you will get around 80 sales. If your book is priced at $2.99, you will get around 2. 6$ /sale, so the total money you earn is 80 x $2. 6 = $164, a profit of 64%. Not bad. Generally, you earn a little more than you invest in total, but the whole idea behind this advertising method is to boost your rank. If you manage to make those 80 sales for 1 book in 1 month + the sales you generally make, you will be able to maintain an overall paid rank of #10,000, which, in many categories, will make you a bestseller.

To create and manage ad campaigns, you need to create an account on Amazon for marketing services. Go to Reports -> Ad Campaigns and you have a dedicated dashboard there (after you sign up).

Chapter 30: Resources

Here, I will include here all the resources you need (I am sorry if some of them repeat, but you can come here for all of them). You can use these resources for anything you need for your books.

Content - You can hire ghost writers to write some articles for you, to rewrite some ideas, add content, or even to write an entire book based on your ideas and indications.

- http://iWriter.com
- http://Freelancer.com
- http://odesk.com
- http://elance.com
- http://Fiverr.com

Cover - Get outstanding designs from $5 up to $500 from the links below.

- http://Fiverr.com

- http://99designs.com
- http://freelancer.com
- http://odesk.com
- http://elance.com

Email services

- Aweber

Ideas - If you don't know what topic to write about, just take a look at these websites.

- http://entrepreneur.com
- http://mindtools.com
- http://amazon.com

Publishing Platforms

- Kindle Direct Publishing (Amazon)
- Smashwords
- Barnes & Noble (Nook)
- iTunes
- Google Play
- FastPencil

- CreateSpace (Amazon)
- Audible ACX (Amazon)

Hire Virtual Assistants

- Facebook Groups
- http://Freelancer.com
- http://odesk.com

Free Websites to submit your book while it's free to get more downloads.

- http://bookfreebies.com
- http://www. rugal-freebies.com
- http://hunt4freebies.com
- http://Kindle-freebies.com
- http://pinyourbook.com
- http://www. heereadercafe.com
- http://www. reebookshub. o. k
- http://igniteyourbook.com
- http://www. readerperks.com
- http://freedigitalreads.com

- http://www. booklister. et
- http://www. ixelofink.com
- http://www. aily-free-ebooks.com
- http://www. ndiesunlimited.com
- http://onehundredfreebooks.com
- http://ereadergirl.com/submit-your-ebook
- http://bargainebookhunter.com
- http://indiebookoftheday.com
- http://bookcanyon.com
- http://snicklist.com
- http://goodKindles. et

Paid Websites (Recommended) for maximum exposure on Amazon

- http://bookbub.com
- http://bookgorilla.com
- http://Fiverr.com
- http://freebooksy.com
- http://ereadersnewstoday.com
- http://thefussylibrarian.com

- http://ebookshabit.com
- http://digitalbooktoday.com
- http://kboards.com

Places where you can submit your book at $0.99 (best for Countdown deals)

- http://bookbub.com
- http://bargainbooksy.com
- http://buckbooks.com
- http://Fiverr.com

Proofreading services

- http://Fiverr.com
- http://odesk.com
- http://freelancer.com

Forums

- http://mobileread.com
- http://kboards.com
- http://worldliteratycafe.com
- Community (KDP Dashboard)

Software

- Evernote
- Microsoft Office
- Adobe Photoshop CS6
- Pages (Mac OS)

1. Best Services that I use and recommend.
   Bookbub – it's by far the number #1 website for promoting eBooks. They have high standards for picking their books, but if you manage to pass their submission requirements, you are GOLD! You can make from 4,000 up to 50,000 downloads just from Bookbub. Prices are high, but results are guaranteed.
2. ***Ereadersnewstoday*** – It is a great value for the price you pay. You get a few thousand downloads for $25 (for nonfiction).

3. **Fussylibrarian** – For $6 you will get from 500 to 2,000 downloads. Fiction books do better on this website.

4. **Fiverr** – There's a guy, BKnights, who guarantees from 100 to 1,000 downloads for your book in 24 hours for only 5$ ($10 for fast delivery).

5. **Freebooksy** – For 80$ (nonfiction), you get from 1,500 to 8,000 downloads. It's expensive, but a good alternative to Bookbub to get additional downloads.

6. **BKnights** – Fiverr – I got 450 downloads for $5, which is excellent. He guarantees 100 – 1,000 downloads. If you don't make at least 100, he will refund the money.

7. **eBookshabit** – For $10, you get a guaranteed placement and your book is shown to over 10,000

subscribers and over 300,000 followers.

8. ***Buckbooks*** – It will give over 10 purchases at $0.99 and will help you increase your rank. This service is free, but you need to have a good quality book.

I use Fiverr for cover creation, proofreading, and editing. Look for Top Rated sellers and you will get the best quality.

Chapter 31: Frequently Asked Questions (FAQ)

1. How do I know that my book will sell?
A: If you do good research on a topic and you promote it well, you will sell it.

2. What if my customers don't like my cover?
A: Make your cover look clean and professional. Highlight the title, use a big font for titles, and vivid colors to catch your readers' eyes.

3. How long will it realistically take until I will start seeing money?
If you write the book in 2 weeks, request the cover, proofread, and do other tasks in another week, promote your book, then you will start making money. In 5-6 weeks after you publish the book, you will start seeing money rolling in.

4. How fast can I make over $1,000/month?

If you follow my guide and keep working hard and release a book every month, I would say 4 to 6 months. If you are lucky and you understood the whole process, you can make that money in 2 or 3 months.

5. How long will my book sell?

It depends on your rank, topic, how well you promote the book, cover, and keywords. If you release high quality books, you can sell it really well for years. If the topic does not have demand, you do not have reviews, and the book is poor quality, in 2 months, it will become "old" and outranked.

6. Can I make a living out of KDP?

Absolutely. Many people are earning a fortune from selling books on several platforms, even if they aren't born writers.

7. Do I need special skills to write a book?

No. You need an average English level and you need to work on daily basis. The errors will be corrected by proofreaders.

8. How long do I need to work each day for this type of business?

If you write 2,000 words a day, you need 2 hours. If you promote a book each day, you need 1 hour. Talking to freelancers and giving them tasks doesn't take more than 2 hours. Uploading and managing your accounts takes 1 hour or less. You will have to work from 4 to 6 hours daily to get results.

9. When can I look to see results in the reports section?

Amazon updates prior six weeks royalties every Sunday and adds a new report on the 15th of each month.

10. How do I get my first reviews?

Tell your best friends about your book, tell your family about the book, submit it to forums, and contact Amazon's top reviewers to have them take a look at your book. Ask them to review it. You will get a lot of reviews when you intensively promote your book and get over 10,000 downloads. For every 1,000 downloads, you will get 1-2 reviews; if you are lucky, probably 3.

11. I published a book and tried everything, why isn't it selling?
Be patient, Amazon's market fluctuates from month to month and from day to day. Analyze results over at least a week.

12. I got a negative review. Is my book horrible?
No. Every book gets negative reviews, even if it Jesus' book.

13. Which are the best days to promote a book?
It's best to promote from Sundays to Thursdays. Avoid Fridays and Saturdays, people are out for a walk, shopping,

people are staying out all night long and won't stay on Amazon.

14. Which months are the best for sales?
Generally, each month is different, but the bestselling months are January and December and the worst are June, July, and August.

15. I got a refund. Why?
People refund books because they bought it by mistake, or they hate it, or a competitor wants to see what you have in your book. It's sad that some "authors" use Camtasia or screen recording software to record the screen, they open Kindle PC and scroll through the book (they copy the text) and once they finish, they refund it. This happens to bestselling books or very expensive books.

16. My sales dashboard isn't updating. Why?
Amazon often has errors and technical issues. Contact them and typely tell them your problem.

17. Should I contact Amazon for any problem?
Yes. They encourage us to do so. Whatever question you have for them, ask.

18. How much money can you make from Audible ACX?
You can make up to 30% of your Kindle earnings.

19. How much money can I make from CreateSpace?
You will make 10-15% of your Kindle earnings. It depends on the topic. Generally, longer books sell better in a paperback format.

20. My rank got better but I didn't make any sales. Why?
If no one sells on Amazon, your rank will get better. You don't have to necessarily sell to rank higher. This is available for small rank increases. If your book is ranked 5,000 in the paid Kindle store,

then you have a problem with the dashboard. Contact them as soon as possible.

Chapter 32: Recap

Based on all the ideas I've put together in this book, I will make a brief recap, so you can know exactly what to do, step by step, to release a book. Check out the previous chapters for detailed information.

Week 1

1. Sign up with Amazon and complete the tax interview.
2. Do market research, find a profitable niche, preferably a topic you have experience in and that you like. Find out who your competitors are, look at their books, and try to make a better one. Plan your chapters before you start writing your book, spread them into multiple subchapters. Learn more about the topic you want to write about, search the web, buy other books, buy courses, and use your

experience; you are going to create a book that has to be the best from your category.

3. Make your own writing plan and stick to it each day. Try to write 1,000–2,000 words every day. Start writing – make sure that your book will have enough content to please your readers and to give them what the title promises. Write at least 10,000–15,000 words or 100 pages for the best results.

Week 2

1. Write your book. Find out the best keywords for your book's title and for the keywords field when you upload the book (7 keywords). Create your title, subtitle, and series name using keywords and benefits. Make your title descriptive and attracting.

2. Create an introduction, conclusion, and a table of contents. Create a

dedicated review page at the end of the book.

3. Promote another book of your own and funnel your readers to your blog, YouTube channel, email list, or social media platforms (when they will be ready).
4. Edit your book by yourself, read it from start to finish, and correct any possible mistakes.

Week 3

1. Create your cover for Kindle and CreateSpace (JPEG & PDF).
2. Proofread your work (send it to proofreaders and editors).
3. Sign up with CreateSpace and complete the same tax interview as for KDP.

Week 4

1. Upload the book on CreateSpace first and wait for approval (1 day). Upload the same book on Kindle. Don't forget to enroll in KDP Select and Kindle Matchbook (if you have created a paperback version). Mail Amazon to link your paperback version from CreateSpace to the Kindle version and ask them to update your page length.
2. Price your book at $0.99 (35% royalty) at first.
3. Acquire 5 reviews – Ask your friends, family, Amazon top reviewers, or other authors to purchase your book and write an **_HONEST_** review. Schedule a 5 day promotion (or at least 3 days in a row) using Free Promotion days.
4. Submit your free book to over 30 websites (48-72 hours before the promotion starts) to get free downloads while it's free. Pay for advertising for additional

downloads. The more downloads you make, the more organic reviews you will get for your book.

5. During the promotion, price your book high ($3.99 – $5.99).
6. After the promotion ends, price the book at $0.99 to make some sales and to rank your book in the paid store. Price your book at $2.99 – $3.

Finish all these steps and make sure to write quality books. From this point, money will start rolling in slowly. If you follow this process, you will make over $100 in your first month.

Repeat the whole process, and release more books.

As soon as you start making some money, create a blog and an email list to funnel your readers.

*** Extras ***

Do you want to learn more about affiliate marketing and Amazon's Associates affiliate program? Do you want to start another online business using Amazon's platform? You may find Amazon Associates very attractive. It's easy to start and it grows more profitable as time goes by. Check out my book about Amazon Associates by clicking the cover below.

You can also check out my other books (more are on their way) by going to my Author page.

If you have any messages related to my books, or if you have any questions, send me a message on Twitter @BookStevens

Write a review

I am constantly improving my books and my work and I am trying to deliver my readers the best quality information. To improve my work and myself as a human being, I need organic reviews to know where I am wrong or where I have made mistakes. Remember, there is no such thing as a perfect book, it needs updates all the time, especially if it's digital. As I mentioned in the previous chapters, reviews are the most essential aspect for selling a book. If this book has been useful to you, please write a review with all your thoughts, it won't take more than 1 minute. If you didn't like something from this book, please contact me and I will try to solve your problem.

Click on the button below to write a review now.

Thank you

Conclusion

I congratulate you for your courage and for your ambition to start your own online publishing business.

Many people talk uselessly and only a few people take action. People like you and me.

If you follow the methods and the tools presented in this book, I guarantee you that you can't fail. If you work hard enough, you can easily earn over $20,000-$100,000/year, but this requires skills, time, perseverance, and dedication.

This isn't a "get rich overnight scheme", it's a unique way of making money online, passively, using the global market place. I want to sincerely thank you for purchasing this book and I feel grateful and honored to teach you what I've learned in over 1 year of publishing eBooks on Kindle.

To your success,

Ryan

www.ingramcontent.com/pod-product-compliance
Lightning Source LLC
Chambersburg PA
CBHW071043290526
45795CB00004B/1299